Sair

Saint Thomas More
Courage, Conscience, and the King

Written by
Susan Helen Wallace, FSP
and
Patricia Edward Jablonski, FSP

Illustrated by
Dani Lachuk

BOOKS & MEDIA
Boston

Library of Congress Cataloging-in-Publication Data

Wallace, Susan Helen, 1940-2013 author.

Saint Thomas More : courage, conscience, and the king / written by Susan Helen Wallace, FSP, and Patricia Edward Jablonski, FSP ; illustrated by Dani Lachuk.

pages cm. -- (Encounter the saints)

ISBN-13: 978-0-8198-9021-4

ISBN-10: 0-8198-9021-9

1. More, Thomas, Saint, 1478-1535--Juvenile literature. 2. Henry VIII, King of England, 1491-1547--Relations with humanists--Juvenile literature. 3. England--Intellectual life--16th century--Juvenile literature. 4. Christian martyrs--England--Biography--Juvenile literature. 5. Statesmen--England--Biography--Juvenile literature. 6. Humanists--England--Biography--Juvenile literature. I. Jablonski, Patricia E., author. II. Lachuk, Dani, illustrator. III. Title.

DA334.M8W18 2014

942.05'2092--dc23

[B]

2013048774

Cover art/Illustrated by Dani Lachuk

All rights reserved. No part of this book may be reproduced or transmitted in any form or by any means, electronic or mechanical, including photocopying, recording, or by any information storage and retrieval system, without permission in writing from the publisher.

"P" and PAULINE are registered trademarks of the Daughters of Saint Paul.

Copyright © 2014, Daughters of Saint Paul

Published by Pauline Books & Media, 50 Saint Pauls Avenue, Boston, MA 02130-3491

Printed in the U.S.A.

STMVSAUSAPEOILL6-110014 9021-9

www.pauline.org

Pauline Books & Media is the publishing house of the Daughters of Saint Paul, an international congregation of women religious serving the Church with the communications media.

1 2 3 4 5 6 7 8 9   18 17 16 15 14

*To the memory of Susan Helen Wallace, FSP
1940–2013*

You wrote love on every page.

Encounter the Saints Series

Blesseds Jacinta and Francisco Marto
Shepherds of Fatima

Blesssed James Alberione
Media Apostle

Blessed Pier Giorgio Frassati
Journey to the Summit

Blessed Teresa of Calcutta
Missionary of Charity

Journeys with Mary
Apparitions of Our Lady

Saint Anthony of Padua
Fire and Light

Saint Bakhita of Sudan
Forever Free

Saint Bernadette Soubirous
And Our Lady of Lourdes

Saint Catherine Labouré
And Our Lady of the Miraculous Medal

Saint Clare of Assisi
A Light for the World

Saint Damien of Molokai
Hero of Hawaii

Saint Edith Stein
Blessed by the Cross

Saint Elizabeth Ann Seton
Daughter of America

Saint Faustina Kowalska
Messenger of Mercy

Saint Francis of Assisi
Gentle Revolutionary

Saint Gianna Beretta Molla
The Gift of Life

Saint Ignatius of Loyola
For the Greater Glory of God

Saint Isaac Jogues
With Burning Heart

Saint Joan of Arc
God's Soldier

Saint John Paul II
The People's Pope

Saint John Vianney
A Priest for All People

Saint Juan Diego
And Our Lady of Guadalupe

Saint Kateri Tekakwitha
Courageous Faith

Saint Katharine Drexel
The Total Gift

Saint Martin de Porres
Humble Healer

Saint Maximilian Kolbe
Mary's Knight

Saint Paul
The Thirteenth Apostle

Saint Pio of Pietrelcina
Rich in Love

Saint Teresa of Avila
Joyful in the Lord

Saint Thérèse of Lisieux
The Way of Love

For other children's titles on the saints, visit our Web site:
www.pauline.org.

Contents

1. Beginnings 1

2. The Scholar 7

3. Soul Searching 13

4. Jane 19

5. New Expectations 25

6. An Urgent Need 29

7. Winds of Change 35

8. God First 43

9. Golden Days 49

10. Keeping the Peace 55

11. One Courageous Voice 63

12. The Undoing of Wolsey 67

13. Dilemma 71

14. Lord Chancellor 75

15. England in Turmoil 81

16. Decisions 87

17. Paying the Price 93

18. Prisoner 97

19. Attempts to Persuade 103

20. On Trial 107

21. Waiting 111

22. The Journey Home 115

Prayer 121

Glossary 123

1
BEGINNINGS

Thursday, February 7, 1478, was cold and cloudy as is common for a winter's day in London, England. Inside the nursery of the More household, a warm fire blazed and crackled. Snug in his cradle, a newborn baby slept under the dancing light.

Sir John More gazed thoughtfully at his son. "You shall surely grow up to be a lawyer, my little Thomas," he whispered, "not a merchant like the grandfather you are named after. No, you will be a barrister—like I am."

As was the custom of fifteenth-century Catholics, Thomas was baptized within a week of his birth. Though the baby was named after his grandfather, he also shared his name with a popular English martyr. Three centuries earlier, Saint Thomas Becket had been born just twenty yards from the More family's home on Milk Street.

Thomas was the second of six children born to John and Agnes More, but only four of their children survived past infancy.

Young Thomas loved being with his older sister and younger brother and sister. The boy had a friendly, cheerful personality, and was always ready for some laughter and excitement. His mother also noticed something special about him: Thomas loved to pray.

Soon enough it was time for Thomas to begin his studies. British schools were known to be very strict, and students were required to work hard. Even though he was only seven, there wasn't much time for fun and games! Since textbooks were so expensive, they were rare. So memorization and discussion were the most popular teaching methods.

"I hope our lively Thomas can adjust," Mrs. More fretted. "Spending long hours in a classroom will be a big change from the life he is used to."

"He will do just fine, Agnes," Sir John assured her. "He's a bright lad, after all."

Thomas and his classmates walked the short distance to Saint Anthony's School on Threadneedle Street. The headmaster, Nicholas Holt, greeted each student at the door. "Good morning, Master More," he said bending to give Thomas a firm handshake. "Welcome to Saint Anthony's."

"Thank you, Sir," Thomas beamed.

Thomas eyed his large classroom. He noticed that some of the other boys seemed nervous and fearful. *There is nothing to be afraid of,* he thought. *This is something new and exciting! And no girls!*

In some ways, Thomas was like his father—quick, clever, and sociable. But he was also very much his own person. Sir John More knew how to charm people into giving him what he wanted, especially those who were considered important and influential. Young Thomas, however, never made distinctions about social class or standing. He enjoyed the company of all his friends, and he valued the unique gifts of each of them equally.

Headmaster Holt was a close friend of John Morton, the Archbishop of Canterbury and Lord Chancellor of England. Sir John More saw this as an opportunity for Thomas to serve in the archbishop's large household. *I want my son to be a success,* Sir John reasoned. *Thomas is intelligent and talented, and there will be many powerful people for him to meet at the archbishop's residence. Even though he's still young, Thomas will be able to make influential social connections there that will be useful to him all his life.*

However Sir John managed it, he was overjoyed when Thomas completed his five years at Saint Anthony's School and was appointed a page, or personal attendant, to Archbishop Morton. Thomas was about twelve when he moved to the archbishop's residence at Lambeth Palace.

Archbishop Morton was a powerful man, but he was also elderly and frail. The damp English climate had never bothered him in his younger years, but now his aches and pains were constant. Nevertheless, he held himself erect and went out of his way to be pleasant and welcoming to the many persons who came to visit him.

Thomas learned his duties well. He was always by the archbishop's side, ready to serve him something at the dinner table or run an errand. On special occasions, Archbishop Morton would invite a group of actors to perform a play while he and his guests enjoyed a leisurely meal. Thomas felt at home enough to join the players in their skits. He would make up his own part and deliver speeches on the spot. On one of these occasions, the archbishop leaned toward his visitors and pointed to Thomas. "Keep an eye on that young page," he advised. "Those of you who may live long enough will see him grow to be a marvelous man."

After two years of service at Lambeth Palace, Thomas was ready to move on to the next stage of his education.

"Thank you for everything, Your Grace," Thomas said quietly as he knelt to receive the archbishop's blessing. "I've learned so much from you. I shall miss you, but I promise I will always remember you . . ."

"I shall miss you, too," the elderly man replied, his eyes welling up with tears. "Go with God, Thomas—and my blessing. Go with God."

"All my friends will have at least a little spending money—"

2
THE SCHOLAR

Moving from London to Oxford University was an adventure. Thomas would be attending Canterbury College at the university. Who knew what awaited him behind those ancient stone walls?

As the carriage driver brought the horse to a halt before the impressive building, Thomas turned to his father. "Sir, in driving through the town I could not help but notice how expensive things are here in Oxford." He proceeded with caution. "Concerning my allowance, Father, I'm wondering if it will be enough . . . under these new circumstances, I mean."

"It is not at all meager if you stay in your room and study," his father replied.

Thomas tried again. "All my friends will have at least a little spending money—"

"Well, not one of them is *my* son," Sir John broke in. "I want to keep you away from frivolous parties and other things that are just a waste of time. Very few young men are able to attend university at all, let alone one like Oxford that has been respected for centuries. This is a chance of a lifetime, Thomas. I expect you to make the most of it."

Thomas had to admit defeat. "Yes, sir," he replied. "I promise to try my best."

Thomas had learned to work hard at Saint Anthony's School. But the life of an Oxford student was even more rigid and demanding.

"I wish we didn't have to get up so early in the morning," Thomas said as he walked into the chapel for Mass at 5:00 AM.

"And I wish we didn't have to wait so long to eat. I'm starving!" whispered one of the other students.

The students at Oxford had no breakfast. Every day, Mass was followed by the first class at 6:00 AM sharp. The first of two meals wasn't served until 10:00 AM. After that, more lectures and tutorial discussions filled the remainder of the day until the final meal at 5:00 PM. All the students were required to be in their rooms by 8:00 PM.

Attending Oxford wasn't going to be easy. But with his usual optimism, Thomas was committed to making the most of his opportunity to learn. In time, he grew to love the simple and disciplined life he lived there.

With few distractions, Thomas began to notice and appreciate things that he might not have paid much attention to otherwise. The fine architecture of the buildings in which he now lived, the gorgeous landscape, the companionship of his friends: these were the things he came to value most. And, as Thomas developed a thirst for knowledge that would characterize the rest of his life, another, deeper fire was beginning to burn within him, too. Above everything else, Thomas longed for greater union with God.

At Oxford, Thomas met Father John Colet who became his spiritual advisor, confessor, and friend. Father Colet was a New Testament scholar and a very dedicated priest. Thomas was impressed by the priest's sincere happiness in his vocation. He admired Father Colet's commitment to God and his Church. "There are so many influences coming at a person," Thomas once confided to Father Colet, "and so many choices to make."

"You're right, Thomas," the wise priest replied. "I have learned to trust that the

Lord will show me my own place in life. I'm sure in time he will do the same for you."

Thomas's father had no doubts about his son's future; he would be a lawyer. In 1494, after just two years at Oxford University, Sir John More transferred Thomas to the system of London law schools known as the Inns of Chancery and Court. Although leaving college studies and the friends he had made hurt him more deeply than anyone ever knew, Thomas threw all his energies into the new endeavor. When he excelled in his introductory courses at New Inn, he was moved on to study at Lincoln's Inn, and finally Furnivall's Inn.

At this last London school, Thomas finished his legal studies and was appointed a reader, or instructor, of the younger students. His lectures were always packed to capacity. "More has a rare combination of brilliance and wit," one professor remarked to a colleague after hearing Thomas teach.

"I only wish I could keep my students' attention the way he does," his friend replied. "You can hear a pin drop when that man speaks."

Faith was as much a part of Thomas's life as his warm personality and intelligence. The priests and monks of two local religious orders—the Carthusians and the Observant Franciscans—were positive role models for the young scholar. Thomas admired their fervor and cheerful witness. He often attended daily Mass and Vespers with them.

Spending time with members of these religious communities raised new questions for Thomas. *Being a lawyer is an honorable profession,* he thought. *At least, being an honest lawyer is! But do I really want to practice law? Is that what God has in mind for me? Perhaps I should consider the life of a priest and or monk instead. . . .*

3
Soul Searching

Thomas needed some guidance and good advice. He went looking for it at the London Charterhouse, the monastery of the Carthusian monks. The Carthusian Order was one of the strictest in the Catholic Church. Living a life of penance and sacrifice was becoming more and more appealing to Thomas, but was it where God was calling him?

The monks offered a wise suggestion. "Thomas, you should come and share our way of life for a while," the abbot invited. "You may continue your law studies while you live here with us, and follow our schedule as closely as you can before taking any vows. Prayer and your experiences here will help you to know if you are called to be a monk."

Thomas was delighted with the invitation. His father, on the other hand, was shocked. "How can this be what you want?" he asked in exasperation. "Think of the career ahead of you . . . of all your years of study . . ."

"I'm not yet sure that I want a monastic life or that God wants it for me," Thomas calmly replied. "The uncertainty has been bothering me for a long time."

"But Thomas, I have put everything within your reach. Consider what you are giving up!" Sir John pleaded.

"That's precisely why I must experience life in the monastery. Please try to understand that I have to find my place, Father. I need to know."

Thomas moved in with the white-habited monks. He prayed with them at the appointed hours throughout the day. He joined in all their acts of sacrifice: rising at midnight to chant the psalms in the darkness of the unheated chapel, fasting rigorously, sleeping on a narrow, hard bed. He even did extra penance for sin by wearing a coarse haircloth shirt that stung and scratched his skin. All the while, Thomas continuously examined both his own soul and the monastic life he was living. In the meantime, he continued to study law.

Thomas knelt alone in the monastery chapel. The late afternoon sun wrapped the ancient church in a golden haze. Thomas raised his eyes to the tabernacle. After living at the Charterhouse for nearly three years, he knew what he must do. *Thank you, Lord,* he prayed. *You have shown me the beauty and nobility of life in the monastery. You have also shown me that it is not my way. I will carry all that I have learned and experienced here in my heart forever. But my calling is to love you as a good Christian husband and lawyer—and perhaps if you will it, as a father. I leave in peace.*

Thomas set up his law office in London. His business grew as quickly as did his reputation for being a just and kind man. Throughout the city, it was known that the young lawyer would never refuse an opportunity to help someone. But beyond that, no one really knew about the countless acts of self-denial and sacrifice that Thomas practiced each day. His most private act of penance was to wear the painful hair shirt he had taken with him when he'd left the monastery. To remind him of Jesus's suffering and love, he wore it next to his skin—

completely hidden from view—for the rest of his life.

Despite his privileged upbringing and education, Thomas was committed to serving those who were in need. When he was elected to the House of Commons in 1504, this aspect of his character made him stand out from many of his less interested peers. As a Member of Parliament, he had his first opportunity to speak out publicly on behalf of the struggling population.

"The taxes are too burdensome for the people," he boldly asserted. "Most cannot afford to pay them. They must be lowered."

Whispers immediately spread through the meeting room.

"I am surprised to see that young More is quite outspoken."

"Yes, but he is right. We all know he is right."

"The king can make do with a little less tax money. We should do something for the people!"

A few hours later, a vote was taken, and a revised tax law was passed. The new tax amount was reduced to just one third of the original. When King Henry VII heard what had happened, he demanded information.

"Who is responsible for this?" he questioned angrily.

"Thomas More, Sire," he was told. "He is one of the newest members of the House of Commons."

The king, burning with rage, plotted his revenge. "I will teach this More a lesson he shall not forget," he vowed. Henry then arranged for false accusations to be made against Thomas's father, Judge John More. The king had Judge John More arrested and dragged off to prison. Though the judge was released a short time later, Henry had made his point; a king can do what he wishes to anyone who dares to oppose him.

4
JANE

Thomas continued to gather around him a growing number of new friends from various walks of life. One of these was a landowner named John Colt, who frequently invited Thomas to his home. Thomas enjoyed his visits with Mr. Colt, his wife, and his family. The food was tasty and the company was lively.

A few of the Colts' daughters were of a marriageable age. And twenty-six-year-old Thomas was quietly attracted to the second eldest, but it was customary that the eldest daughter in a family marry first. *Jane is also a fine young woman*, Thomas thought. *Perhaps if we got to know each other better, we could grow to love each another.*

Seventeen-year-old Jane Colt enjoyed the carefree lifestyle of a wealthy sixteenth-century English family. She was not required to accept any major responsibilities, and she often let afternoons slip away in games and pleasant pastimes with her friends. Jane loved social events. Like the other young women of her day, she had little classroom education. Jane expected to fulfill her life's purpose as most women did—in the role of wife and mother.

I wonder what she thinks of me, Thomas mused. *I'll ask her father's permission to find out.*

Mr. Colt gladly agreed to let the two get acquainted. "Thomas," he exclaimed, "I am happy for you to court my daughter, Jane, and, God willing, make her your wife."

Social customs were very different in those days. The couple was permitted to spend time together only if a chaperone was with them. It wasn't long before Thomas announced his intention to marry Jane. Soon afterward, sometime in 1505, Thomas and Jane were married.

Thomas's daily life didn't change much. But for Jane, getting married changed almost everything. "You don't look very happy, my dear," Thomas noted a few weeks after their marriage. "Is anything wrong?"

Jane's tears flowed out in a torrent. Surprised and speechless, Thomas hugged his distraught young bride, and anxiously waited for some explanation. *Was I wrong to marry after all?* Thomas thought. *Did I do something to make her unhappy?*

Between heaves and sighs, Jane blurted out, "I miss my family, my friends, my games and outings. I cannot cook, Thomas, I don't know how. And I don't know how to be a hostess for your educated friends. I just don't know . . ." Her sobs grew louder.

"Oh, Jane! Let me think about this," her husband said kindly. "There must be a way to make things better for you."

Not knowing what else to do, Thomas paid a visit to his new father-in-law and explained the whole situation.

John Colt chuckled. "I'll go back to the house with you, son. It's time I pay a visit to my daughter."

Jane was thrilled to see her father. She threw her arms around his neck and begged, "Please, please let me come back home!"

Mr. Colt turned to Thomas, "Give us a few moments together, will you, Thomas?"

"Of course, sir," Thomas answered, his face lined with worry and concern.

With that, Mr. Colt led Jane into the adjoining room. As soon as the door closed behind them, Jane realized that her father was not about to take her back to her childhood home.

"You are a woman now, Jane," he reminded her. "You cannot continue to act like a little girl. Surely you realize what a fine man you've married. Can't you see how good Thomas is, how hard working, and respectful? You have a lot to be grateful for," the frustrated father said softly.

Jane stared at her father. Never had she seen him so upset. As tears streamed down her face, she realized that her father was right. Thomas was a good man, and it was time for her to grow into this new stage in her life.

On the other side of the door, Thomas paced back and forth trying not to listen. *I've failed her,* he thought as he waited and prayed. *Lord, help me to love Jane more and better.*

The door finally swung open. The red-faced gentleman who emerged was smiling. Jane had dried her tears. "Forgive me, Thomas!" Jane pleaded as she threw herself into his arms.

"Forgive me, too, Jane. I suppose I just didn't understand. I promise everything will be fine," Thomas quietly soothed. "I'll do more to help you get used to our new life. We'll do things together."

From that moment on, the marriage of Thomas and Jane grew into a true partnership. Their love for each other increased day by day, and they were thrilled when Jane learned that she was expecting their first child. To help her pass the months of waiting for their baby to be born, Thomas gave music lessons to his young wife.

The birth of little Margaret in 1505 was a joyful event. Thomas could never have expected that fatherhood would be such a delight. Cradling his tiny daughter in his arms, he declared, "You, Meg, are the most special child in all of England!"

In the coming years, two more daughters, Elizabeth and Cecily, joined the happy family. Then came a son, John.

Now twenty-two, Jane had blossomed into a contented wife and mother. Her husband and children were everything to her. *How blessed I am to be the wife of Thomas More,* she thought, *blessed indeed.*

5

NEW EXPECTATIONS

Along with his law practice, Thomas continued to study theology, Scripture, and philosophy. There were a handful of other young scholars who shared his interests and pursuit of knowledge. One of these was Desiderius Erasmus, a priest and well-known scholar from Holland. The two men had been familiar with each other's work, but met for the first time at a dinner given by the mayor of London.

"I know who you are," Erasmus announced confidently as he held out his hand. "You are either Thomas More or no one at all."

"And you," replied Thomas mischievously, "are either Erasmus or the devil!"

The Dutchman responded by laughing heartily. Although they differed in their experiences, backgrounds, and personalities, Thomas and Erasmus understood and respected each other. The two became lifelong friends.

Erasmus, a talented author, wrote a biography of Thomas that included his impression of Thomas's physical features and his personality. He wrote, "Thomas is of average height with dark brown hair and blue-gray eyes. He has a healthy and vigorous look about him, and his complexion is light. He seems to be always on the verge of smiling and is calm and serene in spite of the many pressures of his work. He appears to be born for friendship. He has no arrogance. He treats all persons with equal dignity. He likes to dress very simply."

While Thomas was happily occupied with his family, friends, and law practice, changes loomed on the horizon.

The death of fifty-two-year-old Henry VII on April 21, 1509, brought a national sigh of relief. Henry VII had been King of England for twenty-four years. Harsh and unbending, many considered him a tyrant. Henry relied heavily on financing what he wanted from excessive taxation. Ordinary citizens bore the brunt of these fees.

Almost all of England looked ahead with joy and expectation to a new era.

Henry's oldest son, the frail Prince Arthur, had died seven years earlier. That left his next son, seventeen-year-old Henry, the heir to the throne. The young man had a charm about him. He was well educated, talented, and modern in the best sense of the word. Crowned Henry VIII, he appeared to be a promising king.

On June 11 of that same year, King Henry married Catherine of Aragon, a princess from northern Spain. Henry had known Catherine for several years. She had originally come to England to marry his older brother, Prince Arthur. Arthur, however, died just five months after their wedding. Now, because Catherine was the widow of King Henry's deceased brother, the couple needed the permission of the Pope to marry each other. This permission was granted by Pope Julius II. The English people were fond of Catherine and already used to the idea of her being their next queen. Almost everyone was optimistic that the new king and his family would bring renewal and hope to their country.

Thomas was happy to see a new freedom spread throughout England. Then, just when things were going so well politically, personal tragedy struck. In 1511, Jane, his beloved wife, became suddenly ill and died. Thomas's heart was broken and empty. The love of his life was gone. Numb with grief, Thomas sadly hugged each of his four children. Meg, the oldest, was only five. John, the youngest, was not yet a year old. It was difficult and painful to help them understand that they would not see their mother again in this life. *Lord,* Thomas prayed, *may your will be done. But please, I beg you, give me the grace to bear this sorrow with courage and love. And help my children to do the same.*

6

An Urgent Need

Even as Thomas mourned the loss of Jane, he worried even more about the children. In the early morning hours, long before anyone else was up, Thomas was on his knees in his study. *My Lord, help me. I miss Jane so much. We all do. The children are suffering. They need a mother. What shall I do? Please . . . show me.*

Thomas, who was thirty-three at this time, soon realized what he must do. For the sake of his children, he would marry again —and as soon as possible. But who?

Thomas had known Lady Alice Middleton for many years, probably even before he had met Jane. Alice was the widow of John Middleton, a prosperous silk merchant and one of Thomas's friends. Though she was noticeably older than Thomas, forty-one-year-old Alice was an energetic woman and an efficient housekeeper. Her youngest daughter, also named Alice, was about the same age as the More girls.

Thomas met and chatted casually with Lady Alice. A short time later, he paid her another visit, and decided the risk was worth taking. "Alice," he began with some hesitation, "my children need a mother—someone who will love them and raise them as her own." The words sounded so stilted and out of place. Nonethless, he continued. "I know this seems quite sudden, but . . . would you ever consider marrying me?"

A look of surprise crossed Lady Alice's face. Her cheeks blushed. *What an incredible proposal!* she thought. *Heaven knows that Thomas is a good Christian man, but marriage? This is so unexpected. Still, we both want the best for our children.*

Thomas nervously studied the floor. The awkward moments of silence that followed seemed like an eternity. *What will I do if Alice says no?* he thought. Then Alice's serious expression melted into a gentle smile. "I understand your situation, Thomas. After all, I have a child of my own," the older woman replied. "Your children require a mother, not a governess. And my young Alice would be glad to have a father again. Yes, I shall marry you."

Thomas smiled broadly. "Thank you, Alice!" he exclaimed, taking her hands in

"Would you ever consider marrying me, Alice?"

his. "I promise to try my best to make you happy."

Not long after Jane's death, Father John Bouge performed the simple marriage ceremony uniting Thomas and Alice at Saint Stephen Walbrook Church. That fall of 1511 marked a new beginning for the More family.

Lady Alice and her daughter packed their belongings carefully into crates and had them moved to the More home. Alice supervised the unloading and arrangement of all the clothing, household items, and furniture. "Be careful with those dishes!" Alice admonished the servants. "They can never be replaced." Thomas happily watched all the commotion. *I have made the right choice*, he thought. *Alice is just the person we all need. I'm certain it won't take long for love to grow between the two of us. We are already friends.*

❖ ❖ ❖

Busy with his responsibilities as a husband and father, as well as the duties of his law practice, Thomas always made time to pray. He attended daily Mass and prayed the psalms as he had done during his time in the monastery. Because he knew the importance of communicating with God, he set times for family prayer at home. But it was his own example that drew Lady Alice and the children into a deeper relationship with God.

But life in the More household was always exciting and full of surprises.

"Who wants a pet?" Thomas asked one day.

"I do, Father!"

"So do I!"

"Me, too!" the children answered in turn.

The animals, which Thomas brought into his home to the delight of his children, were many and varied. There were puppies, kittens, parrots, ferrets, foxes, and other small creatures. But there were even more exotic animals, too. The children especially loved it when Thomas paraded around the yard with a monkey on his shoulder!

Music lessons also filled the children's days. In fact, Thomas encouraged Lady Alice and even the household servants to learn how to play musical instruments. Although there were excellent schools available, Thomas taught all his children at home. When they were older, he brought in tutors. Thomas was very much ahead of his time. He had his own strong ideas about education and believed that girls—and not just boys—should be formally educated. Meg; Elizabeth; Cecily; Thomas's adopted daughter, Margaret Giggs; and young Alice all studied Latin, Greek, theology, science, mathematics, philosophy, and every other subject alongside their brother, John.

Neighbors, both poor and rich, were always welcome in the More home. When someone he knew was in difficulty, Thomas frequently brought his children with him for a visit. At some point during the conversation, he would often quietly slip a packet of money into the needy person's hand. "It is not enough to know the Gospel," he would remind his children. "We must *live* it."

7
Winds of Change

The More household was not the only one undergoing changes. The palace of the king was also going through a time of adjustment. Young Henry VIII was learning to rule England.

"It is especially important that the king, as inexperienced as he is, be surrounded by good and upright advisors," Thomas often insisted to his colleagues. "The future of our country depends on this." It wasn't long before Thomas found himself more involved in politics.

In May of 1515, he was sent as one of England's ambassadors to Flanders (now part of the Netherlands). Problems were brewing between the English and Flemish merchants. Though the negotiations were expected to last sixty days at the most, Thomas was away for nearly six months.

The weeks in Flanders passed slowly, and Thomas missed his family terribly. To pass the time, he wrote what would become a well-known book, *Utopia*. In it, Thomas described a fantasy kingdom in which everything was perfect. His purpose was to give an insightful critique of his society as it was and propose a path for England's future. The book was immediately popular when it was published in 1516. People still read it today.

The tense situation with the merchants in Flanders was finally resolved in October of 1515. In the end, Thomas's sense of humor and fairness enabled him to earn the trust of the Flemish and successfully conclude very delicate negotiations. He and his fellow ambassadors joyfully sailed back home to England. Thomas was grateful to see his family again. His law practice had been neglected while he was away and work had quietly piled up on his desk.

Meanwhile, Bishop Thomas Wolsey, an ambitious man, had been chosen by Pope Leo X to become a cardinal. There was a great celebration when the cardinal received the large red hat, which symbolized the honor of his office. Cardinal Wolsey was delighted and made himself very visible in the court of King Henry VIII. Thomas observed Wolsey's behavior with concern, but had little to say about the situation. He simply added the new cardinal to his prayers.

One of the first court cases that Thomas tried after returning home to England was an important one. The accusation was that a papal ship had been illegally docked at Southampton Port. Thomas was called to defend the Pope's nuncio, or representative. It was a very public case—even King Henry and Cardinal Wolsey attended the proceedings. Thomas's brilliant defense not only won the case, it also gained him the attention and respect of people in powerful positions.

That kind of attention was what Thomas's father had hoped for him, even when he was a child. It was the usual way to become successful and influential in England at the time. Nonetheless, Thomas was surprised to learn that he had been appointed to the king's advisory council, called the Council of the Star Chamber. By 1516, Thomas's friendly nature and many achievements had drawn him into a circle of highly influential men. But the skillful lawyer was beginning to feel vaguely uncomfortable. Success, and all that came with it, had never been the focus of Thomas's life. *So many politicians and ambitious men set their sights on life at the king's court,* Thomas reflected . . . *Let them have it! I only ask to use all you have given me to serve, Lord,* he prayed, *and that His Majesty may surround himself with just and honest advisors.*

❖ ❖ ❖

The eve of May 1, 1517, found London in an ugly mood. Hostility against foreign merchants living in the city was running high. "These foreigners are stealing our business!" the English merchants cried. "With Italians, Flemish, French, and Germans everywhere, how will we feed *our* children?" The voices grew louder and angrier.

The crowd milling in the streets was quickly growing into a mob. At first, they only cursed and shouted. But soon enough some actual fighting broke out, and riotous acts of violence against the foreign businessmen spread through the city. London city officials asked Thomas to intervene. Risking his own well-being, Thomas went out to reason with the angry mob. His courage and concern for their plight was not wasted.

Order was finally restored in the early morning hours of May 2.

King Henry, concerned about his friendship with the royal families of other nations, was determined to teach a lesson to the people of London. "Prepare gallows in several areas around the city," he ordered his armed guard. "Choose thirteen of these rabble rousers and publicly hang them." The royal order was carried out without hesitation. The rest of the rioters—between 300 and 400 men and boys, and eleven women—were arrested and sentenced to the same fate.

The mayor and his aldermen were shocked by the king's cruel punishment. It seemed to them that he had overreacted to the whole situation. Again, they called for Thomas. "You must lead the delegation of men we are sending to His Majesty to plead for mercy for the offenders," the mayor insisted. "Perhaps you can reason with the king."

"I'll try," Thomas promised. "But a king may be more difficult than a crowd," he added.

Dressed in black as a sign of mourning for those condemned to death, Thomas and his companions approached the king's throne. Henry was not about to give in. "To my mind, they should *all* be hanged," he told Thomas coldly. "But go and present your case to the Lord Chancellor, Cardinal Wolsey."

"As you instruct, Sire," Thomas humbly replied, bowing to the king.

After hearing Thomas present the delegation's request, Cardinal Wolsey arranged a great outdoor ceremony in which the prisoners, wearing ropes around their necks, knelt before the king and pleaded for mercy. Even Queen Catherine fell on her knees before her husband. "I beg you, my Lord," she cried with tears in her eyes, "pardon the prisoners for my sake."

Still the king stubbornly refused mercy to the offenders. Finally, after many more appeals and a speech by Cardinal Wolsey, King Henry backed down. "I, Henry, King of England, pardon you," he dramatically proclaimed to the prisoners, "but let such a thing never happen again!" The relieved crowd broke into applause and praise of the king. The whole episode seemed like a triumph for Henry and Cardinal Wolsey.

"They're cheering us, Wolsey!" the king exclaimed, both puzzled and delighted.

"They are, indeed, Sire," Cardinal Wolsey remarked. "But it seems to me they ought to be cheering Thomas More. Except for his efforts, this all may have ended quite differently."

Both men knew that Thomas was the real hero. If he hadn't intervened with the crowds in the first place, the riot would have flared even more out of control. And if he hadn't pleaded for the king's mercy, hundreds of prisoners would have been executed, and Henry would have lost the respect of his people just as his father had.

❖ ❖ ❖

"Perhaps More could be of further use to us at court," King Henry mused. "Perhaps."

Due to his victory in the papal ship case and his role in calming the London riot, Thomas was called more and more often into the king's service. Because he was fair-minded and sensible, Thomas was someone Henry knew he could trust. The only one excited about his popularity with the king, however, was Thomas's wife, Alice.

"You should be happy to have the king's confidence, Thomas. After all, it is far better to rule than be ruled," she quipped.

"Ah, Alice, now you speak the truth," Thomas retorted with a chuckle. "For I have yet to find you willing to be ruled—and I suspect I never will." They both laughed heartily.

8

GOD FIRST

Although Thomas's life at home and in politics was very demanding, he always made time for God. On most days, Thomas rose at 2:00 AM, washed, dressed, and went down to his study. Quietly closing the door behind him, he began his daily time of prayer and spiritual reading, which usually lasted until 7:00 AM. Thomas often flipped open his Bible randomly and read whatever he had turned to. On this day, his glance fell on a passage of Saint Paul's Letter to the Ephesians:

Watch and be careful how you live;
   be not foolish, but wise.
Make the most of today's opportunity,
because these days are evil. . . .
Try to understand what the will
   of the Lord is.

Thomas meditated and prayed over Saint Paul's advice. *I love peace and want to choose it always, Lord. But if trouble comes, help me to be wise and fair, and above all, faithful to you.*

Soon enough, Thomas needed the graces for which he had prayed.

"I am being sent to Calais, France," he announced to Alice one evening.

His wife looked up from her needlework in surprise.

"Our group of delegates has been commissioned by the king," Thomas continued. "We will negotiate treaties between the English and French merchants and try to deal with the problem of piracy."

"The king is entrusting that to you, Thomas?" Lady Alice asked. "How long will you be away?" she fretted.

"I have no idea, but I promise to return as soon as possible," Thomas assured her.

Thomas remained in France for three months. Though he was not happy to be away from home, one consolation of the trip was seeing his old friend Erasmus again. But there was a more important benefit to the mission that Thomas did not expect: King Henry's attention and approval. "It seems that Thomas More is someone I can trust," the king noted to himself. "Perhaps it would serve me well to make use of him in matters of greater importance."

❖ ❖ ❖

A few years after Thomas's return from France, excitement stirred the More household when Meg, Thomas's oldest daughter, married young William Roper in 1521. His joy for Meg, however, was cut short when he learned a shocking secret not long after the wedding. Through his contacts with some German merchants, Thomas's son-in-law had been introduced to some current heresies that had divided the Church there. The new ideas of these "reformers" had convinced William to abandon his Catholic faith. Thomas was stunned.

To make matters worse, Master Roper was becoming very vocal about his thoughts on religion—so vocal in fact, that he was summoned to Cardinal Wolsey's office. "I have heard that you are spreading ideas contrary to the Faith," said the cardinal. "What do you have to say for yourself?"

"What you've heard is true," the young man bluntly admitted. "But these ideas are not a scandal to believers in Christ, only to those who claim the authority of Christ in the Church."

The cardinal's face reddened and his temper flared. "Roper, I have no patience with this disobedience and lack of reverence for the Church. But because you are Thomas's son-in-law, there will be no prison or fine *this* time. Consider yourself duly warned."

Thomas spent many long hours trying to reason with his confused son-in-law. He patiently and respectfully answered all of William's objections. But it was like talking to a wall. In a sense, there was a real wall between them—a *spiritual* wall. Through it all, William stubbornly held onto his sincere, but mistaken beliefs.

Meg realized how deeply her father was hurting, but she was caught in the middle. She saw the pain in his eyes, and heard the worry in his voice, but there was little she could do. "I cannot reach William, Meg," Thomas sadly admitted. "I have reasoned and argued with him on points of religion, and given him my poor fatherly advice, but none of this has called him home. And so, I won't argue or dispute him any longer. I shall only pray to God for him."

Meg nodded in silent agreement. *Father amazes me,* she thought. *I don't know how he manages to be so spiritual when he spends so much time with people whose only desire is to grow in wealth and power.*

Thomas continued to offer up prayers and sacrifices for his daughter and her husband. It wasn't too long before William quietly and humbly returned to the practice of his Catholic faith. He never strayed from it again.

Thank you, my Lord, Thomas prayed when Meg gave him the good news. *Our faith is certainly a gift—and one never to be taken for granted. Make our hearts strong in your truth, Lord.*

9
GOLDEN DAYS

King Henry was delighted with Thomas's able service as a personal advisor and lawyer. In the same year of Meg's marriage, 1521, the king honored Thomas with knighthood. From this point on, he was called *Sir* Thomas More.

"What a wonderful distinction, Thomas!" Lady Alice exclaimed in delight. "It is, of course, high time the king made you a knight."

Thomas could only smile. He was determined to remain humble in his service to everyone, including King Henry. That is why he still wore the penitential hair shirt beneath the rich robes of his office. It reminded him that he was just a poor sinner in need of God's mercy.

When Charles V, King of Spain, arrived in England for a visit in June of 1522, Thomas handled most of the arrangements and even gave a welcoming speech. This required that he work side by side with King Henry. In the course of their collaboration, the two men became close friends. Thomas began to know his king in a more personal way.

The following year, Thomas was named Speaker of the House of Commons by King Henry and Cardinal Wolsey. These were "golden days" for Thomas and his family. His success made it possible for them to move to a large house in Chelsea, surrounded by a garden and farm. His property bordered the Thames River. Although it was close to the city, it had all the greenery and seclusion of a country estate. Here Thomas was an attentive host to a steady stream of guests—the most famous of whom was the king himself.

King Henry visited Thomas at home on several occasions. Unannounced, and full of the unpredictable, he would tap on the door and take delight at the servants' surprise. But more than anything, Henry enjoyed the genuine warmth with which Thomas always welcomed him inside.

On this particular day, the sun was warm and the More's garden was in full bloom. King Henry and Thomas strolled casually among the flowers and shrubs totally immersed in the friendly conversation they were having. Lady Alice, the younger children, and Meg and Will watched the scene in awe, their noses pressed against the windowpanes. "I can't believe it!" one of the children whispered with excitement. "The king has his arm draped over Father's shoulder!"

"I didn't think anyone was allowed to touch the king," another one of the children said, a bit puzzled.

"They aren't, dear," Lady Alice replied quietly. "But it seems that King Henry has decided to bend the rules himself. He must think very well of your father. Very well, indeed."

After King Henry left, the whole family clustered around Thomas. Will expressed what everyone else had been thinking. "How impressive it is, Sir, to see you on such friendly terms with His Majesty!"

"I have no reason to be proud, Will," Thomas replied kindly, "for I know that if my head could win Henry a castle in France, I would certainly lose it."

❖ ❖ ❖

The English Parliament was convened in the spring of 1523. The most important point on the agenda was Cardinal Wolsey's desire to raise certain taxes to 800,000 pounds in order to provide the king with the money he desired. Rumors of complaints and grumbling quickly reached Wolsey. Seeing the need to act without delay, he promptly dispatched a message to the Parliament: "I shall come in person to speak to the assembly."

As the Speaker of the House of Commons, Thomas was well aware of how afraid the Members of Parliament were of Cardinal Wolsey. Everyone knew that the cardinal had the power to make or break any of them politically—and personally. While many might have otherwise opposed him, they all had families to support. The threat of Wolsey's retaliation made it difficult for them to be true to their own principles.

On the appointed day, Cardinal Wolsey and all his attendants strode pompously into the meeting chamber. "What questions and complaints do you have for me now?" Wolsey demanded, glaring at the men assembled before him. The silence that followed was deafening. Wolsey stared coldly at the Speaker's podium where Sir Thomas stood. "Your Grace," Thomas said quietly, "it might not be to your advantage to be here in person right now."

Wolsey angrily stormed out of the hall. Due to Sir Thomas's patient mediation, Wolsey eventually did get the tax raise he wanted. Still, the cardinal was upset. *Thomas grows in fame and popularity,* he thought to himself, *and I am becoming dependent on him. This will not do.*

On September 14, 1523, only two years after his election, Pope Adrian VI died. The ambitious Cardinal Wolsey, hoping to be selected as the next Successor of Saint Peter, sailed to Rome to participate in the conclave in which a new pope would be chosen. *This time,* he thought, *I will surely be elected.* But he was in for a bitter disappointment. The cardinals, under the inspiration of the Holy Spirit, chose Giulio de Medici, who took the name Pope Clement VII.

The humiliated English cardinal returned home. Those who lived and worked with him couldn't help but notice that from that point on Cardinal Wolsey was tense and scowled more frequently than ever.

10

Keeping the Peace

Thomas was saddened to see that some well-known and educated Catholics had left the Church and were spreading false and confusing ideas about the Catholic faith. William Tyndale and John Frith were former Catholic priests. Simon Fish and Christopher Saint-German were lawyers. Caught up in Martin Luther's Reformation movement that was sweeping Western Europe, these men had now bitterly turned against Catholicism and the Church.

In order to correct the errors that they were spreading, Thomas put his pen to work. This time, he wrote in English rather than Latin. Thomas used calm reasoning as well as humor in the essays he wrote to defend the Catholic faith. He was a master at presenting difficult theological debates in ways the common layperson could understand. His writings clarified matters for many people searching for answers in those confusing times.

Upheaval within the church had a shattering impact on what had been, up until then, a unified society. But tension was also on the rise due to some actions and attitudes of King Henry VIII. As the years passed, Henry had become more and more impressed with his own royalty. People bowing, flattering him, and feeding his ego didn't help. Unfortunately, the natural, unassuming ruler of earlier years had all but disappeared. Everyone noticed that the king had changed. Some used it to their advantage. Others, like Thomas, were sorry to see that it was not a change for the better.

In many ways, King Henry was at war with his own weaknesses and fears. Ambitious men did whatever was necessary to gain his favor for their own purposes. Clever women sought his attention and approval, even tempting him to be unfaithful to his wife, Queen Catherine. Because he himself craved attention, Henry was more than willing to give them all what they wanted, even if it involved doing something immoral or unjust.

More personally, Henry and his wife, Queen Catherine, had drifted apart. One of the primary reasons was the problem of an heir to the throne. The royal couple had

had six children, including three sons. Only one daughter, Princess Mary, however, had survived. The tradition of the English people was to have kings—not queens—rule the country. Yet it was not likely that Queen Catherine, at her age, would ever have another baby. Even if she did, there were no guarantees that any child would be a son or live into adulthood. Henry was deeply concerned about not having a male heir to the throne. The future of the House of Tudor, his royal family, was at stake. Attentive to these concerns, Henry distanced himself from Queen Catherine and Princess Mary.

Through the long winter of 1526 to 1527, the atmosphere at court grew tenser and less secure. Thomas, who spent extended periods there because of his service to the king, wished for more time with his own loving family. *Lord,* he prayed, *what is happening to the royal family is complex and difficult, but you can do all things. Please help the king.*

One of Queen Catherine's closest servants, her maid-in-waiting at that time, was twenty-year-old Anne Boleyn. Her father, Sir Thomas Boleyn, was an important man at King Henry's court. He was one of the first to notice Anne's way of attracting the king's attention.

Anne was ambitious and fearless. Although she was not born into royalty, she had no trouble considering the possibility that, through a few clever moves, she might eventually become the queen. Meanwhile, King Henry began showing affection for her in many little ways.

By the spring of 1527, it was clear that the king was very unhappy. "Is there a problem we may help you with, Sire?" his advisors often asked, being careful not to pry.

The answer was always the same. "I am very preoccupied with a serious matter," the king would mumble. "It is my *great matter*," he would add with emphasis.

Henry's "great matter" involved his marriage to Queen Catherine. He had convinced himself that the fact the couple did not have a surviving male child to become the next king was a sign that his marriage to Queen Catherine was not pleasing to God. Henry planned to ask the Church to declare that his marriage to Catherine had never really been a valid Christian marriage after all. With an annulment from the Pope, the king would be free to marry someone else—someone young enough to give him a son who could be the next King of England.

Henry became more and more anxious to find a way to separate from Catherine. "I never should have been permitted to marry her at all," he protested. "Catherine is the wife of my dead brother Arthur. The Holy Bible does not allow such a union. It is not a marriage!" the king proclaimed, raising his voice. Still, nothing could change the fact that Henry had asked the Pope for permission to marry Catherine in the first place. And the Pope had granted it. No one had reason to question the marriage before.

Henry's public humiliation of his wife, Catherine, was painful to watch. Those in the king's service began to feel pressure to turn against the queen. The royal marriage became the topic of court gossip and discussion. It wasn't long before Thomas realized that underneath all the discussion and debate was another reason King Henry wanted to annul his marriage. The king had become very attracted to Anne Boleyn. Thomas prayed even harder, *Lord, keep the king from destroying his own soul. Bring him back to his wife and his faith!*

During that same year, King Henry sent Cardinal Wolsey's secretary to Rome to ask the Pope for special permission to marry again *without* an annulment. A short time later, the secretary returned, empty-handed. Cardinal Wolsey asked for a private audience with the king to explain the outcome. Instead, he was led to the great hall where he found King Henry with Anne Boleyn at his side. The cardinal stopped, puzzled. "Come in," Anne demanded rudely. "The king is here."

Cardinal Wolsey stumbled through his report about his secretary's failure to obtain the Pope's permission. The king was not at all pleased.

Life at the king's court was filled with uncertainty and anxiety. From Rome, Pope Clement VII decided that a trial regarding the legitimacy of Henry and Catherine's marriage would take place in England. Two cardinals would be responsible for the trial proceedings: Cardinal Wolsey and Cardinal Lorenzo Campeggio from Rome. Cardinal Campeggio would act as the Pope's personal representative.

As months passed, the ailing Pope Clement VII died and the new pope, Paul III, asked Cardinal Campeggio to stall the proceedings. "In time," he reasoned, "Henry will become disenchanted with this ambitious woman. When the king returns to his senses, he'll be finished with Anne Boleyn."

Nearly two years passed, but the king did not tire of Anne. She—and not Catherine—remained at his side. So, in June of 1529, the trial began.

11
ONE COURAGEOUS VOICE

"Catherine, Queen of England, enter the court!"

A nervous hush fell over the assembly, which included all the English bishops. With a rustle of silk, the suffering queen entered the hall, scanning the crowd for a friendly face. Catherine had proven many of her own talents. In fact, she had been the first female ambassador in Europe. She knew that her marriage to Henry was valid and that their daughter, Mary, should succeed King Henry on the throne of England. But Catherine also knew that England had not been ruled by a queen in centuries. A male heir was very important to the king. With renewed grief for the untimely deaths of the infant sons she and Henry had lost, Catherine curtsied and then knelt before her husband. "I have been a good and loyal wife to you for twenty years, my Lord," she declared in halting English. "I put this matter to your conscience." Turning slowly to face the assembled bishops, she then proclaimed in a steady and determined voice, "To God I commit my cause."

Majestically, and with complete self-control, the queen rose to her feet and left the hall. Realizing the emotional impact of Catherine's words, Henry, set out to persuade the bishops by reminding them that this "grave matter" of his involved his conscience. "Do you not agree, my Lords, that for the sake of conscience I should put aside Queen Catherine? For it is my conscience that tells me I should never have married my brother's widow. Surely, there is a life of prayer awaiting her at a convent somewhere?" the king pleaded.

After some stressful moments, Archbishop Warham, the spokesman of the whole assembly of bishops, rose to his feet. "Yes, Your Highness, we agree."

Suddenly, a lone voice rang out. "No! 'Whom God has joined together, let no man divide.' You do not have *my* consent to separate from the queen!"

All heads turned to the dissenter. It was John Fisher, the Bishop of Rochester.

"Look at this!" the king angrily shot back, waving a piece of paper. "Is not this your seal on a letter recommending that my request for an annulment be sent to the Pope?"

Fisher glanced furiously around at his fellow bishops.

"I assure you, Your Highness, it is not! At least I did not put it there. I would never consent to assist you in obtaining an annulment. It is against my conscience."

"I affixed Bishop Fisher's seal to the document, Sire," the embarrassed Archbishop Warham quietly admitted.

A long silence followed, punctuated only by Henry's nervous pacing. "No matter!" the king finally bellowed. "We will not trouble to argue with you, Bishop Fisher, for you are only one man."

The trial went on. At least forty witnesses who supported the king came forward to speak in favor of allowing him to "follow his conscience." The voice of Bishop Fisher was drowned out. Finally, Cardinal Campeggio motioned for silence. "I am suspending these proceedings," he firmly announced. A murmur ran through the astonished crowd. "As Queen Catherine has requested, this trial will continue in Rome."

"There is little opposition to the wishes of the king, Your Holiness," Cardinal

Campeggio later wrote to Pope Paul. "No one comes forward in the queen's name any longer. I have closed the trial in London. It must be completed in Rome."

King Henry was furious. *The Church has failed me,* he thought angrily. *But I am king in England. Wolsey will pay for this!*

12

The Undoing of Wolsey

The trial to grant King Henry an annulment had failed. Cardinal Wolsey was white with fear. Everyone knew that this had been a kind of trial for him, too—a test of his influence and power. On October 9, 1530, the king removed Wolsey from service as Lord Chancellor. The news spread quickly. Church laws had been upheld in the matter of the king's marriage. The king, however, had been bitterly disappointed.

As the representative of the Church of Jesus Christ, it was Cardinal Wolsey's duty to stand up for the law of the Church. But to do this now, in defiance of King Henry, would mean prison and death. Somewhere along the line, Wolsey had chosen to be more loyal to the king than to his faith. He had become very attached to the power and riches he enjoyed as a result of those choices. This choice would be no different from those that had brought Wolsy to this point. The aging cardinal threw himself on his knees before Henry. "I beg you, Sire," he pleaded. "Give me a second chance. I am sure we can come to a satisfactory agreement about your problem."

"No!" Henry shouted. "I have had enough of you. Leave me at once and return to your home."

Cardinal Wolsey was exiled to his country home in Esher. Crowds lining the streets of London echoed the king's displeasure and screamed "Traitor!" at him as he left the city.

"Thomas, did you hear the good news? Wolsey is removed!" said one of the king's younger and less experienced servants at Court.

"To me it can only be sad news," Thomas replied. "It is always painful when a man falls so far from what he should be. But perhaps this distance from the king will bring Wolsey closer to God."

"I can't say I'm sorry to see him go," the young servant remarked.

"You may find yourself wishing for him someday. Remember, none of us yet knows what kind of man will replace him as the king's chancellor," Thomas observed cautiously.

Back at home, Wolsey waited anxiously. He expected trouble to erupt at any moment. He didn't have long to wait.

Answering his door one morning, the cardinal came face to face with the Earl of Northumberland. "My Lord," the latter announced, "I am here to arrest you for high treason. Gather your things for you are to stand trial in London. We must leave right away."

By the evening of the third day of the journey back to the city, the cardinal was seriously ill. The traveling party stopped at Leicester Abbey. The hospitable Augustinian monks offered to care for Cardinal Wolsey and immediately put him to bed.

Sensing that death was near, a much-humbled Wolsey made a confession of the sins of his whole life and received the Anointing of the Sick (called Extreme Unction at that time) and *Viaticum*, his last Holy Communion. As his many evil deeds flashed through his mind, he had deep regrets. *If I had served God as diligently as I have the king, God would not have given me over in my old age,* Wolsey thought to himself. Then, without any special attendants or comforts, Cardinal Wolsey died.

The monks sang a beautiful funeral Mass for the man who had spent his life in pursuit of power, splendor, and luxury. But no monument was erected to mark Cardinal Wolsey's tomb. His example had not been one to imitate or remember.

13
Dilemma

Sir Thomas continued to spend long hours with the king, advising him on legal matters. He was always very careful, however, to avoid anything to do with the king's marriage. *I must not get involved in the king's quest for an annulment,* Thomas thought. *I have a family that depends on me. But maintaining the proper distance is easier said than done.*

"Thomas," the king said one afternoon when they were alone, "about my *great matter* . . ." Thomas shuddered. "Would you contact the bishops of Durham and Bath? I'd like you to learn their insights concerning my marriage dilemma."

Thomas felt his body stiffen and his face flush. He knew he was treading on dangerous waters. Henry's request was risky not only for him, but for the bishops he had mentioned. Remaining as calm as possible, Thomas answered, "Your Highness, the two bishops you've mentioned are good, honest, and educated. I know, however, that they would not consider themselves authorities on the sacrament of Matrimony. I am confident that they would refer me to the early Church Fathers, to Saint Augustine and Saint Jerome for example, to search for your answer."

Thomas paused and looked kindly into the face of his monarch. Henry was scowling. Their eyes met. The king smiled faintly. "Oh, go ahead then and search the Church Fathers, Thomas," he grudgingly agreed.

Thomas let a sigh of relief escape him as he continued on to the next matter on their agenda. He was safe for now, but how much longer could he evade the king's questioning *him* about the annulment? How long would he be able to keep his own opinion on the matter to himself? He didn't know.

The long day had finally ended. Thomas wrapped himself in his woolen cloak and headed for the castle's large doors. *There is only one way to handle this situation*, he told himself, *remain true to the faith, trust in God, and speak as little as possible of the king's affairs.* Guards pushed the heavy doors ajar, and Thomas stepped out into the crisp evening air. He walked the short distance to the river's edge. Thomas's heart lifted as he pictured his home and waiting family. A small boat stood ready for passengers, even though the hour was late. The boatman helped Thomas to board and sit, then began to row. The steady rhythm of the oars on the water soothed Thomas's frayed nerves. He could feel the tension in his body lifting and his eyelids growing heavy.

The ride was far too short this night. Sir Thomas disembarked and walked slowly along the silent road toward his home. Within minutes, Meg and her husband, Will, ran up to meet him. Meg matched steps with her father and wrapped herself in part of his wide cape. Will made some small talk as they walked along. Meg knew that her father was pleased to have their company.

The trio entered the house, had supper with the rest of the family, and went quietly to bed. The night would pass quickly, Thomas knew. As he lay there, between wakefulness and sleep, Thomas wondered. *How many more peaceful nights will I be able to spend with my family if the king becomes angry with me?* He would rise early the next morning to pray for courage, enough to face whatever lay ahead.

14
Lord Chancellor

The king's court was as filled with rumor and gossip as usual. People were engaged in guessing, observing, and waiting impatiently for information about political happenings. The latest topic centered on whom the king's new chancellor might be. Cardinal Wolsey had not made a very good one, people agreed. Soon the king himself would appoint the cardinal's successor.

"Does he have to be a clergyman?"

"Could the king appoint a layman, someone educated, honest, and loyal to the post?"

"Perhaps, but he probably should be a lawyer..."

There were as many opinions as there were speculators.

But everyone did agree on one thing: having the right person in this powerful position was especially important—even vital—for the good of the country now. The chancellor was the king's chief adviser and an important judge. He was considered second in authority only to the king himself.

In good times and in bad, his role was extremely important.

It was not much of a surprise to many at court when Sir Thomas was summoned by the king on October 25, 1530. Henry got right to the point. "Thomas, I want you as my new chancellor." Thomas's jaw fell open for a moment. "Do you know who recommended you?"

"I cannot imagine, Sire," Thomas quietly responded.

"Our former Lord Chancellor, Wolsey," the king answered appearing amused at Thomas's shocked expression. "Yes, it was Wolsey himself."

King Henry asked the Duke of Norfolk to organize a glorious celebration for Thomas's installation, since the two were close friends. Amid much ceremony and speechmaking, Henry presented the Great Seal of the Chancellor's office to Sir Thomas with the traditional admonition, "First look upon God, and after God, upon me." These would prove to be prophetic words for Thomas.

Sir John More, Thomas's ninety-year-old father, was proud of his son's success. Lady Alice was thrilled. Thomas's many friends, along with a few adversaries, congratulated

"First look upon God, and after God, upon me."

him. Thomas sincerely thanked them all. Then, he turned his heart to God. *I have never desired to be chancellor or be placed in any high position of influence. Lord, make me worthy of this honor and of you,* he prayed. With his usual dogged determination, Thomas plunged into his new responsibilities.

There was an impressive backlog of cases awaiting the Lord Chancellor's attention. Some had been pending for as long as twenty years. One after the other, Thomas gave the people their day in court. His personal interest meant so much to those who hoped for justice.

Sir Thomas heard court cases every weekday. He handled and concluded issues fairly and according to the law. Finally, the day came when his court officers informed him that there was no more unfinished business to handle. That was when a little rhyme sprang up among the people of London:

> *When MORE some time had Chancellor been,*
> *No more suits did remain;*
> *The same shall never more be seen*
> *Till MORE be there again.*

The qualities that made Thomas successful in the courtroom were his patience and honesty. For him there was no such thing as an insignificant case. Each one—no matter how small—received the chancellor's full attention.

One afternoon, an old beggar woman appeared before Thomas's bench. She stepped up and shyly began her story. "My little dog has run away, Your Lordship. He has been taken in by a wealthy lady who now claims that the dog belongs to her. When I tried to speak to the lady, her servants refused to let me see her."

"And what is this lady's name, my good woman?" Thomas kindly asked. "Perhaps the servants will let me speak to her."

The old woman's cheeks flushed with embarrassment. "She is the wife of the Lord Chancellor," she softly replied.

"Really! Then this matter should be easily resolved," Thomas reassured her.

Sir Thomas sent for his wife and the dog. When Lady Alice arrived, he asked her to stand at one end of the room and the beggar lady to stand at the other. Gently picking up the squirming dog, Thomas walked to the center of the courtroom and set it on the floor. "I want each of you ladies to call the dog by name," he instructed. "He is sure to go to his proper owner."

As both women began to call, the puppy sprinted happily toward the poor woman. She affectionately hugged him. "The dog is yours, Madam," Thomas observed, "You are free to take him home." Pressing a gold coin into her wrinkled hand, he added quietly, "I would like you to have this as well."

"Thank you, Your Lordship," the woman tearfully murmured. Feeling overcome by Thomas's goodness and generosity, she turned to Lady Alice and carefully placed the little dog in her arms. "You keep him, my Lady," she instructed, "and take good care of him."

15

ENGLAND IN TURMOIL

Being in almost daily contact with King Henry, Sir Thomas realized just how tired and anxious the king had grown over the matter of his marriage. Thomas tried tactfully to keep his working relationship as calm and pleasant as possible without commenting on Henry's personal life. But things were rapidly going from bad to worse.

By July of 1530, King Henry had left Queen Catherine permanently. In fact, Anne Boleyn had boldly moved into the queen's apartments. The whole situation was very unpopular throughout England, and when Anne appeared in public, crowds sometimes hissed.

There were other serious problems too. By threatening revenge if they didn't agree, King Henry had persuaded most of the English clergy that he, not the Pope, was "supreme head of the Catholic Church in England." On May 15, 1532, a document titled "The Submission of the Clergy" was presented to Henry by the Archbishop of Canterbury. By signing "The Submission," members of the English clergy swore not to make a move without royal consent and approval. The Catholic Church in England had come under the authority of the king. As the king's right-hand man, Thomas had a very important decision to make.

He rose early as usual to pray for God's guidance. *Lord, it seems I will not be able to serve two masters any longer. There is no real choice here; I know what I must do. Just give me the courage to do it, Lord, and remember to keep my family in your care.*

The next day, May 16, 1532, Sir Thomas More resigned his office as Lord Chancellor. Lady Alice sat in stunned silence. The entire household listened anxiously as Thomas unfolded a story of political and romantic intrigue, a story of a man—a king—who, like men of all times, had to choose between God and the world. "King Henry has chosen the world," Thomas sadly concluded, "but because he is the lawful King of England, his choice will have a devastating impact on all his subjects."

"What will happen to you now, Thomas? What will happen to us?" Alice asked in a quivering voice.

"Things will surely be different," Thomas replied with a faint smile. "But whatever happens, I must follow my conscience, Alice, and side with God—even if it means incurring the wrath of the king."

Sir Thomas could have resumed his law practice. Instead, he took up his pen again, but now he wrote full-time. Most of the English clergy were so perplexed and worried about the state of affairs in England that they scarcely thought of Martin Luther's teachings against the Church and the heresies raging in Europe. But Thomas did. During this time, he wrote a series of books defending the true Catholic faith. Together, they totaled almost half a million words!

The More family also noticed how often Thomas began to speak about the joys of heaven, the pains of hell, and the martyrs—especially the martyrs who died bravely and willingly for their Catholic faith. These were fast becoming his favorite topics of conversation.

Now that his income had been drastically reduced, Sir Thomas could no longer maintain his large staff of servants. But before letting them go, he made sure to find each of them a new job. The servants were sorry to leave the joyful More household.

Only the jester, however, was able to joke about it.

"Chancellor More is Chancellor no more," he chanted before breaking down and bursting into tears. The Mores' jester was sent to continue his merry-making in the home of the mayor of London.

When the family was left with only the plainest of possessions, Sir Thomas made light of it and kept his usual smile. But Meg knew the sorrow and pain that were eating away at his heart. "I worry for Alice and for you my children," Thomas confided to her. "Sometimes I am awake an entire night thinking, fearing what the king in his anger might do to all of you." He reached out and took Meg's hands in his own. "Remember this, Meg, we need faith. A person could be utterly destroyed without it."

❖ ❖ ❖

In August of 1532, William Warham, the Archbishop of Canterbury, died. King Henry nominated Bishop Thomas Cranmer to take his place. The Pope approved the choice, and Cranmer was made archbishop. Then Parliament gave Archbishop Cranmer the power to settle the "problem" of the king's marriage. The English clergy went along with this decision. Soon Archbishop Cranmer announced that Henry's marriage to Catherine was invalid. It was clear the king had orchestrated everything to get the annulment he wanted. Thomas sensed that a series of events had been set into motion.

On January 25, 1533, King Henry secretly married Anne Boleyn. That April, he publicly announced that Anne was his wife and would be crowned Queen of England. The news sparked both sadness and confusion.

"How terrible for Queen Catherine!" many remarked.

"Does the king think he can have *two* wives?" some asked.

By the time Anne was crowned, she was expecting a baby. As former Lord Chancellor, Thomas was expected to participate fully in royal events. But Sir Thomas did not attend Anne's lavish coronation ceremony in June of 1533. The king took his absence as a personal insult and became very angry. *Soon enough*, thought Thomas, *I will be the target of his revenge. I cannot escape it forever.*

The situation became even more complicated for Thomas on March 23, 1534, when the Vatican declared Henry and Catherine's marriage to be true and valid. Now the sides were clearly drawn: the archbishop and the King of England against the Pope and the Catholic Church. Thomas knew that it wouldn't be long before everyone would be forced to choose between them. "Soon," King Henry boasted, "I will be pope *and* king in England."

Things were moving swiftly. A week later, the English Parliament passed "The Act of Succession," which declared that Anne's children would be heirs to England's throne instead of Queen Catherine's daughter, seventeen-year-old Princess Mary. Anyone who refused to accept this law could be accused—and convicted—of treason. The penalty was death.

Queen Catherine wrote a passionate letter to the Spanish ambassador asking him to appeal to her nephew, Emperor Charles of Spain, for help. Only the threat of an invading army could put an end to the terrible injustices she was suffering. The emperor received the urgent message from his aunt, but had to consider his political situation carefully. Charles decided that his own position was not strong enough to send an army to defend the rightful Queen of England. As a result, the rescuing army never came.

16
DECISIONS

King Henry was not satisfied with Parliament's passage of the Act of Succession. So, he established a commission that would require all bishops, priests, and deacons, as well as more important government officials to proclaim their agreement with the Act of Succession. These same leaders were also required to take an Oath of Supremacy, which recognized the king—and not the Pope—as the head of the Roman Catholic Church in England. By taking the Oath of Supremacy, churchmen and government leaders renounced their union with the Pope and declared that he had no more power than any ordinary bishop did.

On April 12, 1534, Sir Thomas was summoned to appear before the king's commission. He knew that he would be asked to take the dreaded oath. He also knew that he could not compromise his faith in good conscience. Thomas prayed. *I am in your hands, my Lord. This moment has been a long time in coming, but I knew it would come. You, Lord, know my weakness well. Be with me!*

That morning Thomas prepared himself by going to Mass and receiving Holy Communion. It was difficult for him to say goodbye to his family that day. He alone knew that he might never see them again as a free man. Lady Alice and the rest of the More family had no idea how dire the situation was. Only Meg did. The sadness she saw etched on her father's face caused a stream of silent tears to slip down her cheeks.

Will accompanied Thomas through the quiet streets to the dock. The journey to Lambeth Castle was made in a small boat. There was complete silence except for the steady splash of the oars. Even this sound went unnoticed by Thomas who was deep in thought. He reviewed the oath in his mind, measured past events, and anticipated future outcomes. Soon enough, his wrinkled brow became smooth again, and Thomas appeared almost cheerful. He had decided what to do. *Silent—I shall remain silent*, Thomas thought to himself.

"Son," Thomas said turning to Will, "I thank our Lord the field is won."

Will, who had no idea of the seriousness of Thomas's predicament, responded, "Sir, I am very glad."

Leaving the wharf, the two men continued on to the castle. At the entrance, Thomas embraced Will. Turning back as the gates closed behind him, he pleaded, "Pray for me." Will lingered there a few moments. He was suddenly very much afraid.

Sir Thomas was brought before Archbishop Thomas Cranmer, Lord Thomas Audley, and Thomas Cromwell. The commission waited in apprehensive silence as he entered the room. They knew him, and he knew them. Every man in the room understood what he could expect from all the others. Thomas greeted each of them graciously. He was outwardly calm. "Sir Thomas," the archbishop began sternly, "we have called you here to pleadge your loyalty to the king in all his concerns."

As a well-trained lawyer, Sir Thomas grasped exactly what was happening and the significance of what was about to transpire. He had reflected on the price this meeting could demand of him and, above all, what it could mean for his family. Thomas struggled to control his runaway thoughts. *God is with me,* he inwardly repeated. *God is with me.*

"I understand. May I look over the Act of Succession?" Thomas asked cordially. The commission members knew that he was already fully aware of what the Act involved, but they could not deny the request. They handed Thomas the document. Thomas read it carefully then set it down on the desk before him. "I am ready to swear to the Act of Succession, my Lords . . ."

"Good man, Thomas!" Lord Audley broke in. "A sensible decision indeed."

Thomas waved his hand in protest. "I have not finished, though" he quietly replied. "I will swear to the Act, but my conscience will not allow me to take the Oath of Supremacy."

An awkward silence filled the room. "We will inform you of those who have already taken the oath," Archbishop Cranmer finally ventured. "That might guide you."

The names of bishops, priests, and members of the House of Commons who had sworn the oath were then read aloud. Coming to the end of the long list, the three commission members waited expectantly for Thomas's response.

"My Lords," he said calmly, "what these other men have done does not change my thinking. They must answer to their consciences, and I alone must answer to mine. This law, however, punishes only those who speak against the king's new title as head of the Church," Thomas reasoned. "I have said nothing about the subject—nor will I."

The three men whispered nervously among themselves. They knew the punishment awaiting Thomas if he refused to take the oath, and they were afraid of the uproar that might occur if they were forced to put a well-known, honest man like Thomas More to death. "We wish to give you a chance to reconsider, Sir Thomas," Cromwell asserted. "Go into the castle garden and think about the importance and consequences of this matter. Stay even for a few hours while we administer the oath to others who are waiting. We shall speak again when you come inside."

"As you wish, my Lord," Thomas responded with a slight bow of his head.

The spring day held no beauty for Thomas as he paced the paths of the garden. He knew that his life and the well-being of his family depended on his willingness to take the oath. He also knew that he would be putting his soul in grave danger if he purposely sinned against his conscience and publicly accepted Henry as the head of the Church in England. Thomas was not searching for a decision. He already knew what his answer must be. Instead, he was searching for the strength to bear the consequences that would surely result from his decision— torture, death, and the suffering of his family. *Please, Lord,* he begged, *give me grace and courage to do what I know is right.*

17
Paying the Price

As he circled the garden, Thomas became aware of much coming and going. He looked up to see a group of priests filing into the castle to take the oath. *How calm and cheerful they appear,* he thought sadly. *Do they not realize what they are about to do? How can they so easily abandon the faith? My God, have mercy on us all!*

Just then, a lone priest was led out of the castle, his face drawn and ashen. Thomas shielded his eyes from the sun. He strained to recognize the cleric. *It's Father Nicholas Wilson,* he realized in shocked dismay, *the king's friend, and his former confessor.* Thomas felt a wave of dread wash over him. He shivered in spite of the mild temperature. *Father Nicholas must have refused to take the oath,* he realized. *He's on his way to the Tower of London. If this is how Henry treats such a close friend and confidant, what will he not do to me?*

All too soon, Thomas found himself once again before the commission. "What do you say now, Sir Thomas, about the oath?" Archbishop Cranmer persisted.

"I say nothing, Your Lordship," Thomas replied in a steady voice. "I will swear to the Act of Succession, but I cannot take the oath."

"Thomas, think well about what you are saying," warned Lord Audley.

"I can assure you that it is all I have been thinking about," Thomas answered.

After trying in every way to convince Thomas to change his mind, the frustrated commissioners turned him over to the guardianship of the abbot of Westminster Abbey. They may have hoped that by doing so, his life would be spared. Thomas remained at the abbey for four days. In the meantime, a rumor had spread that King Henry had decided to set Thomas free. Then, the one voice still capable of influencing Henry spoke to him.

"Sir Thomas has never approved of our relationship, my Lord," Anne Boleyn angrily reminded the king. "Remember how he ignored your invitation to my coronation. He has offended us both," she insisted. "You should find him guilty and make him an example to all of England."

The king was tired and frustrated. He wearily rubbed his temples.

"Enough!" he finally snapped back. "He shall go to the Tower!"

On Friday, April 17, 1534, Sir Thomas was led to Traitor's Gate of the Tower of London. Opening the door of a cold stone cell the regretful jailer mumbled, "I am sorry for the miserable accommodations, Sir."

"There is nothing to worry about, my good man," Thomas responded, trying to joke. "If you find that I am not pleased with the place, you can always throw me out."

At first, Thomas was allowed certain special "privileges"—pens, ink, paper, some favorite books, a daily walk, and the chance to attend Mass. Immediately he began his first letter to Meg. *Since I have come here in order to remain true to my conscience,* he wrote, *I trust that God, in his goodness, will look after you and our family, and, with his gracious help, make up for the lack of my presence among you. . . .*

Involuntarily, his fingers suddenly lost their grip on the pen, and ink pooled from the fallen quill tip. *What can I write?* Thomas agonized. *How can I make them understand why I must choose the faith, even if it means death in this situation? Tell me what to say, Lord.*

Thomas blotted the ink spot and picked up his pen again. *I may tell you, Meg,* he continued, *that they have committed me here for refusing to take the Oath of Supremacy, an oath that is not in agreement with English law. Therefore, they will not be able to justify my imprisonment.*

Even as he wrote these words, Sir Thomas realized that, no matter what, King Henry was in complete control of his life. *In the end, nothing will matter. The king will do with me as he pleases,* Thomas mused, *just as he pleases.*

18

PRISONER

As a prisoner in the Tower of London, Sir Thomas had long hours in which to ponder his situation. *Freedom is within my grasp*, he thought, *if I could bring myself to take the oath. But what a foolish exchange it would be to lose my soul. Instead, I'll surrender my earthly freedom for eternal freedom in heaven and find comfort in the passion of Christ.*

In the days ahead, Thomas began to write down his reflections on the sufferings and death of Jesus. The topic became more and more real to him in the midst of his foul-smelling, damp cell. Being able to pray, to pen letters to his family and friends, and to write about his Savior gave Thomas the courage to accept his terrible situation with peace.

And through it all, he continued to wear his hair shirt, as an act of penance. Perhaps Thomas offered this sacrifice to God to unite him even more with the sufferings of Jesus. Or, he may have done so for a special intention known only to himself.

Meg was allowed to visit her father. The first time that she actually entered his cell and realized the true danger Thomas was in, she burst into tears. "Sign the oath as the others did, Father," she begged, "and come home to us again. I cannot stand seeing you like this. Do it for me . . . please!"

Thomas tried to explain; there was so much he wanted to say. But the words died on his lips. Only after Meg left did he break down, filling the cell with muffled sobs. *Lord, help me to help her understand,* he prayed.

Almost immediately, Thomas began a letter to Meg, trying to capture the thoughts of his soul. "None of the terrible things that might happen to me touch me as grievously as seeing you, my child, in such a pitiful state," he wrote. "And this grief is greater when you attempt to persuade me about the thing that I have—out of respect for my own soul—already given you so clear an answer."

When Lady Alice was permitted to visit in order to try to convince her husband to take the oath, she begged him to return to their home in Chelsea. Thomas surveyed his dank cell and quietly answered, "Wife, isn't this house just as near to heaven as my own?"

"Sign the oath as the others did, Father."

The weeks stretched into months. Thomas Cromwell, the new confidant of King Henry, was annoyed by the fact that Thomas More was still in prison. He was determined to find a way to force Sir Thomas to give in to the commission.

When Cromwell went to visit Thomas, he was shocked to find that the former Lord Chancellor was allowed paper, pen, and ink. "Who let you have these?" Cromwell haughtily demanded.

"Please," Thomas begged, "let me keep them. They are of great consolation to me."

"No!" Cromwell snapped, "Permission is denied." And he had the items removed. Later, even Thomas's books were confiscated. With nothing more to read, Thomas spent his time in prayer and meditation.

Cromwell's resolve to break Thomas's resistance hardened even more. As time wore on, Thomas's punishment was intensified. "I apologize, Sir Thomas," the jailer announced one morning, "I have been told that you may take no more walks outside your cell." He paused and lowered his head, adding quietly, "The priest chaplain is no longer allowed to visit you either."

A sad sigh escaped Thomas's lips. *Please, Lord,* he prayed, *be my counselor now.*

Without pen and paper, Thomas could not continue writing his reflections on Jesus's sufferings. He would soon be walking to his own Calvary with the Lord. Though the written work would remain unfinished, Thomas would live it out.

Thomas was not alone in his sufferings. One day a hastily scrawled note was delivered to his cell. Its shaky handwriting was from a man who had been confined to the Tower on the same day Thomas had— Father Nicholas Wilson. Realizing that a death sentence was drawing closer each day, the priest desperately wondered if there was a way to compromise and take the oath without endangering his soul. Thomas, managing to find a scrap of paper and a piece of coal, kindly wrote back without any hint of criticism, "I beg Our Lord to give you good luck . . . I shall leave every other man to his own conscience and, with God's grace, will follow my own. Remember me in your devout prayers, and I will remember you in mine."

A while later, Thomas read, with a heavy heart, a final message from Wilson: "I have decided to take the oath."

❖ ❖ ❖

Thomas Cromwell arranged to let Meg continue to visit her father every now and then—not out of compassion, but with the hope that Meg could convince Thomas to change his mind and take the oath. Executing a man like Thomas More, respected by nearly everyone, could turn the people against the king. Cromwell knew that an angry ruler was one thing, and an angry mob was quite another.

During one of these visits, when father and daughter were deep in conversation, the shuffle of footsteps echoed in the hall. Looking through the small cell window Thomas saw several of his good Carthusian monk friends along with a parish priest being led out of the Tower to their execution.

"Look at those holy men, Meg," he said in a voice hoarse with emotion, "they have spent their lives for God. Your father could never match their penances and prayers filled with such love of God. I am not worthy to follow them."

Meg clung to her father and wept.

Silence will not protect me much longer. It is only a matter of time, Thomas realized. *My God, have mercy on my poor soul.*

19

ATTEMPTS TO PERSUADE

As strange as it might seem, it is quite certain that King Henry VIII really didn't want to put Sir Thomas More to death. Though he desperately wanted Thomas to take the Oath of Supremacy and recognize him as head of the Catholic Church in England. Henry loved Thomas as a friend. He kept trying every means imaginable to persuade him to change his mind.

All of London's most influential men were called, one by one, to visit Thomas's cell. They tried every clever approach, but Thomas's answer was always the same. "The law is like a two-edged sword. If I should speak against it, I shall bring about the death of my body. If I should consent to it, I shall bring about the death of my soul."

Even Lord Audley, one of the original members of the commission who had sent Thomas to prison, stopped to see him. "Thomas, others are imitating your example," he began in a low voice. "They, too, are refusing to take the oath. You are causing us much grief."

"I have never tried to influence anyone against the oath," Thomas responded calmly. "I am in charge of my own conscience alone. I cannot judge anyone else. I have remained silent and have said nothing against His Majesty."

Another courageous man who had refused to take the oath was also imprisoned in the Tower of London at this time—John Fisher, the Bishop of Rochester. Pope Paul III had raised Bishop Fisher to the office of cardinal, hoping to persuade the king to spare his life.

Henry VIII dispatched his cruel reply to the Pope, "I will so arrange things that if the bishop wears the red hat, he will have to do so on his shoulders, since he will have no head to put it on."

Cardinal Fisher and Sir Thomas More were now Henry's principal concerns. The two men were continually examined and cross-examined. Every trick imaginable was used to entice them to deny that the king was head of the Church in England. Then, the men who dared to oppose the king could be charged with treason.

Richard Rich, an agent of the king, was sent to Cardinal Fisher. "What you tell me will be held in complete secrecy," he promised. "The king wishes to know your personal opinion for the good of his conscience."

"Tell the king," the cardinal answered weakly, "that I am certain that he is not and cannot be by the law of God supreme head of the Church in England."

Rich triumphantly returned to the court with the needed evidence to convict the elderly man of treason. The trial in Westminster Hall was only a formality. The verdict was pronounced long before the courageous cardinal ever stepped into the courtroom. He was sentenced to death. The execution was scheduled for five days later, on June 22, 1535. After his torturous imprisonment, Cardinal Fisher was so thin and ill that one witness described him as, "Death in a man's form, using a man's voice."

As the executioner readied his tool, Cardinal Fisher was offered a pardon if he would agree that the king was the supreme head of the Church in England. Ignoring the offer, and turning to the crowd of spectators, the frail cardinal begged, "Pray that I will be faithful to the Catholic faith to the end."

The axe, poised above the cardinal's neck, did its cruel work.

"The people must learn what happens to those who disobey me," Henry boasted. He had Cardinal Fisher's body thrown into a shallow grave and his head hung on London Bridge for everyone to see. The cardinal's head remained on the bridge until July 6, when it was removed to make way for the king's next victim.

20
On Trial

Richard Rich, the Solicitor General who had betrayed the holy cardinal, now focused all his attention on Sir Thomas. He tried to trick Thomas into publicly denying the king's right to be head of the Church in England, but Thomas saw through him and evaded all Rich's attempts.

Soon enough it was Thomas's turn to be tried in the English court. The trial was set for July 1, 1535. Dressed in a rough robe, Thomas was led on foot through the most populated streets of London to Westminster Hall, the site of the courtroom. Usually, contempt would be shown for any man who dared disobey the king. But there was no hatred shown that day. The crowds looked on in awe and admiration as the broken man passed by. After fourteen months in a damp prison cell, Thomas's health was poor. Although he was only fifty-seven, he could hardly take a step without faltering, and he struggled to keep up with the procession. His once broad shoulders were now terribly stooped, and he was shockingly thin. His beard had grown scraggly and long.

"We do not agree with this, Sir Thomas!" some in the crowd shouted. "We promise to pray for you!"

Others sobbed at the terrible shock of seeing one of the most beloved men of England, the champion of the common man, reduced to such a state. But while his body was broken, Thomas More's gifted mind was as keen as ever.

Upon entering the courtroom itself, Thomas discovered that he knew every man on the jury. How they dreaded this moment, this trial, more than any other. It was said that Thomas More did not merely look at a man; he looked *through* him. None of the jurors looked forward to that soul-searching glance.

As the accusations were read, Sir Thomas calmly and brilliantly cleared himself on every charge. The trial was dragging and sympathy for the prisoner was mounting. Sir Thomas was so weak that he was allowed to sit while he gave his defense. But Richard Rich knew just how to achieve the result he wanted. He lied on the witness stand and committed perjury, presenting to the court a statement Thomas had never made. "I heard it with my own ears," Rich testified. "'Parliament,' Sir Thomas said, 'does not have the power to make the king head of the Church in England.'"

A shocked murmur ran through the courtroom. All in attendance knew that Sir Thomas was far too intelligent to have made such a statement. They knew that Rich was lying. And yet, out of fear of the king, the jury declared its verdict just fifteen minutes later: "We find Sir Thomas More guilty of treason."

The whispering continued until the judge banged his gavel. "The sentence," he announced "is death by decapitation."

This was the moment Thomas had feared. He had not been afraid of the sentence. He had feared only that he might lack the courage to accept it. But the grace had come when it was needed.

Thomas's steady gaze searched the faces of his judges. "I forgive you," he said quietly. "I forgive you as Blessed Stephen forgave Saul. And just as now both are holy saints in heaven and shall continue there as friends forever, so I trust and pray that, though your Lordships have been on earth my judges of condemnation, we may meet hereafter merrily together in heaven."

Tears were their only reply.

21
WAITING . . .

A procession formed to take the condemned man from the courtroom back to the Tower. As a symbol of what was to come, the executioner's axe was carried ahead of Thomas with its sharp edge facing him. Sir William Kingston, the official in charge of the Tower of London, directed the sad spectacle. Crowds of sympathizers lined the streets. As they moved in the direction of the prison, Thomas's young son John bravely pushed his way through the line of guards. Kneeling at his father's feet, he buried his head against his body and begged for his blessing. Thomas traced the sign of the cross on his forehead. Kingston wept so loudly at this scene that Sir Thomas had to console him. "I will pray for you and your dear wife," Thomas assured. "Be of good cheer. We will meet again in heaven where we shall be merry forever."

When the group arrived at the gate of the prison, some of Thomas's friends and family members were waiting. Meg ignored the crowd, the jailer, and the guards. She saw only the prisoner in his ragged woolen robe.

"Oh my Father!" she cried, breaking through the tight barrier of soldiers, swords, and halberds surrounding Thomas. "My dear Father!" Meg flung her arms around Thomas's neck and kissed him over and over. This moment took more courage for Thomas to face than any courtroom verdict.

"Whatever I suffer, even though I am innocent," he whispered caressing her face in his hands, "is allowed for a good reason by God. Do you believe that, Meg? You must believe." Thomas pressed her tightly to himself. It was time to enter the Tower. Meg felt his grasp weaken. "Go now, Meg, You must go."

Hardly able to see through her tears, she stumbled away before suddenly turning and rushing back. Again, she kissed her father as many times as she could. Thomas was so moved, he could no longer speak. Most of the spectators were now in tears.

"We must continue on, Sir Thomas," Sir Kingston urged in a quiet voice. "It is time."

❖ ❖ ❖

Thomas spent the final six days of his life praying, fasting, and writing. His rough piece of charcoal was busily engaged in scribbling farewell notes.

Lady Alice was allowed to visit one final time. She carried home the last letter Thomas wrote, along with his hair shirt. Thomas's note was addressed to Meg. Although it was never completed (Lady Alice was probably asked to leave before Thomas could finish writing), it read in part, "Goodbye my dear child. Please pray for me, and I shall pray for you and all your friends that we may happily meet in heaven."

A few days later, the cell door swung open. The visitor was Sir Thomas Pope, a friend of Thomas's and a member of the king's council. "Sir Thomas, His Highness wishes me to inform you that you will die at nine o'clock this morning," he solemnly announced.

"I heartily thank you for your message, Master Pope," Thomas replied. "And I thank the king for having confined me to this place where I have had the time and space to prepare for a good death. I will not fail to sincerely pray for His Grace here and in the next life."

"There is one more thing, Sir Thomas," the councilor added, looking a bit embarrassed. "The king requests that you do not speak many words at the time of your execution."

"Thank you for this warning, Master Pope," Thomas amiably responded, "for I had been planning on making somewhat of a speech. Of course, I will obey the king's wishes. However, there is one favor I wish to ask of His Grace."

"And what is that, Sir Thomas?"

"That he allow my daughter, Margaret, to be present at my burial."

Pope fought back his tears. "His Highness has already decreed . . ." he stopped to clear his throat, "that your wife, children, and friends may attend your burial."

Thomas smiled in relief.

Thomas Pope couldn't help himself. He broke down and cried.

22

THE JOURNEY HOME

Later that morning, Sir William Kingston came to lead Thomas on his last journey. It was July 6, 1535. As was the custom at executions, Thomas was allowed to wear his own clothes. He carried a small red cross in memory of the sufferings and death of Jesus.

As the prisoner began his difficult journey to the place of execution, a woman pressed near and offered him some wine to lighten the agony. Thomas smiled and gently refused. "Jesus did not accept wine on his way to Calvary, and neither will I. But I thank you for your kindness."

"Sir Thomas," another woman called out, "you were unfair to me when you were chancellor."

"I remember your case well," Thomas responded. "You see that at this moment I am on my way to my death. If I had to judge your case again, I would not change anything. Be content. You were fairly treated."

A man shouted, "Master More, do you remember me? You helped me to avoid suicide. Please pray for me now. I am so unhappy and downcast." Thomas stopped and turned toward him. "Go your way in peace, and pray for me," he answered kindly. "I promise that I will pray for you."

Mounting the scaffold on that sultry July morning, Thomas didn't think of himself as a martyr. In fact, he even did his best to make light of it. In Thomas's mind, there was nothing glorious or extraordinary about what was now taking place. He was ending his life as he had always lived it—according to his conscience.

The crowd had hoped to hear some last words of insight from the condemned man. But the sheriff explained that King Henry had asked Thomas to be brief. As always, Thomas obeyed. Looking about at the crowd, he said in a faint but steady voice, "Please pray for me. I am dying for the faith of the Holy Catholic Church. I die the king's good servant, but God's first."

Thomas then knelt and began to pray aloud the words of Psalm 51, "Have mercy on me God in your kindness . . ." Finishing the prayer, he rose to his feet. Now it was the custom for the executioner to kneel

ILLUSTRATION 5

"I die the king's good servant, but God's first."

before the prisoner to beg his pardon and ask his blessing. When this was done, Thomas kissed the axe man. He also placed a gold coin in his palm saying, "Today, you will give me a greater benefit than any mortal man could ever give me."

Thomas knelt again. The executioner raised his axe. With one powerful swing, Thomas's head was severed from his body.

The king was informed as he and Queen Anne were playing cards. Henry threw his cards onto the table. "You!" he shouted, pointing angrily at the queen. "You are responsible for Thomas's death!" He rushed out of the room and wasn't seen again for hours.

Sir Thomas's body was taken to the Church of Saint Peter in Chains within the Tower of London. There it was buried in the presence of some of his family.

Thomas's head, however, was hoisted on a pole at London Bridge as a warning to anyone who would dare oppose the king. It replaced the head of Cardinal John Fisher.

❖ ❖ ❖

Like the death of Saint Thomas Becket, an English archbishop who had been martyred centuries earlier for standing up to King Henry II for his faith, the deaths of Cardinal Fisher and Sir Thomas More made an enormous impact on the people of their day. Sadly, however, their deaths did not bring peace to troubled England.

Henry VIII ordered the execution of Anne Boleyn just one year later. Although he eventually had six different wives, none of them gave birth to a surviving male heir. After Henry's one son died at the age of sixteen, both Princess Mary and Princess Elizabeth claimed the throne. Catherine's daughter, Mary, reigned for a brief time, and then she died. Anne Boleyn's daughter, Elizabeth, ruled England and Ireland as queen for the next forty-four years.

Under Henry VIII, England cut its ties with the Roman Catholic Church, and became a Protestant nation. The royal government during his reign and in the years that followed claimed ownership of all Church property and began an era of persecution against Catholics in England, Ireland, and even North America that would last for centuries.

Four hundred years later, many continued to be inspired by the courage and sacrifice of Sir Thomas More and his friend

Cardinal John Fisher. The two martyrs were proclaimed saints by Pope Pius XI on May 19, 1935.

They share the same feast day each year on June 22.

Prayer

Saint Thomas, you were really courageous. You could have given in to the king, kept your high position, and saved your life as many others did. But you chose to follow your conscience and obey God's law instead.

Today, more than ever, followers of Jesus need to stand up for what is right—even when everyone else is telling them that they're wrong. Sometimes it's easier to keep quiet and just go along with things that are against God's law. But that's not how I want to live, Saint Thomas. Help me to be like you. Help me never to be afraid to follow the teachings of Jesus and to live the faith that I have received as a gift from God.

Thank you for also showing me how to care for the poor, treat everyone fairly, and forgive those who have wronged me. It can be very hard to forgive someone who's hurt me. But you found the grace to do it.

Saint Thomas, patron of all those who bravely stand up for what is true and right, please give me your courage, faith, and love. Show me how to form a right conscience and do what is best for my soul. Amen.

Glossary

1. **Abbey**—a monastery under the direction of a Father Abbot or Mother Abbess who serves as the spiritual leader of the monks or nuns.

2. **Aldermen**—members of a city council. According to differing customs, an alderman could be chosen by his fellow councilors or elected by the voters.

3. **Annul**—to annul a marriage means to declare that for a serious reason or reasons, the marriage did not fulfill the requirements of Church law from the start, and therefore was never a Sacramental Christian marriage. An **annulment** is the name given to the official declaration that a marriage is invalid.

4. **Anointing of the Sick**—the sacrament by which Jesus gives spiritual comfort, strength, and at times physical healing to a person who is seriously ill due to sickness, injury, or advanced age. The Holy Spirit, through this sacrament, also forgives sin and heals the soul. The anointing of the sick

is administered by a priest using blessed oil on the sick person's forehead and hands.

5. **Chaperone**—someone who accompanies young people in order to make sure that their behavior is morally sound and appropriate.

6. **Clergy**—men who have been specially ordained to serve as deacons, priests, and bishops in the Catholic Church.

7. **Conclave**—the private meetings at the Vatican in which the cardinals gather to elect a new pope. During a conclave, cardinals are not permitted to communicate with anyone else.

8. **Confessor**—a priest who celebrates the Sacrament of Reconciliation for others and absolves them of their sins.

9. **Conscience**—the judgment our mind makes about whether what we are about to do (or have done) is (or was) good or bad. Our will makes decisions according to the thoughts and ideas we already have. This is why it is so important for us to form a right conscience according to God's will. We can know God's will by the natural laws that God has placed in our hearts and through

the truths that our Catholic faith teaches us. Unfortunately, we can also form a wrong conscience when we do not pay attention to or obey God's laws.

10. **Decapitation**—an execution performed by cutting off a person's head.

11. **Gallows**—a wooden structure used for execution by hanging.

12. **Hair shirt**—a shirt, made of goat's hair or some other coarse material, worn as an act of penance.

13. **Halberd**—a common weapon of the fourteenth and fifteenth centuries. It consisted of a spiked blade of an axe mounted on a long pole so that it could be used on horseback.

14. **Headmaster**—a man who serves as the principal of a school, usually a private school.

15. **Heresy**—the denial or the act of publicly teaching against a truth of the Catholic faith that has been revealed by God in Sacred Scripture or sacred tradition.

16. **Inns of Chancery and Inns of Court**—the traditional education system for train-

ing young men to be lawyers. Throughout the history of England, lawyers have been divided by their function into *barristers* and *solicitors*. A barrister represented a person's interests in high court. A solicitor worked directly with a client and had the power to act in the place of his client.

17. Jester—in medieval times, a person hired to entertain a king or a nobleman. The work of the jester included clowning, juggling, singing, playing music, and telling jokes and riddles.

18. Lord Chancellor—one of the most important English government officials who was in charge of the royal seal which the king used to seal documents in place of signing them. Originally, the chancellor was always a priest, who also served as the king's chaplain and spiritual and political advisor. In addition to his duties at the king's court, the chancellor acted as a judge.

19. Meager—small or insufficient.

20. Monastery—the place where friars, monks, or nuns live as a community, dedicating themselves to a life of prayer. The term is usually applied to the residences of religious orders which are cloistered, that is live in separation from the world.

21. **Oath**—a solemn declaration in which one calls on God either as a witness that one is telling the truth or that one definitely intends to do what he or she is promising.

22. **Page**—a young male servant in medieval and renaissance times. Pages still serve in a few places today, such as the United States Congress and in Canada's House of Commons.

23. **Piracy**—a general term referring to acts of theft or violence committed at sea. Persons who commit piracy are known as pirates.

24. **Quill**—a large bird feather which was used as a pen during medieval times. The end that had been closest to the bird's body was cut to a sharp point and then dipped in liquid ink to form a writing instrument.

25. **The Reformation**—a time of social upheaval from about 1517–1648 in which some persons, upset with problems within the Catholic Church and the sinful actions of some of its leaders and members, introduced changes and divisions that split the

Church. These led to the founding of numerous Protestant churches and denominations no longer under the authority of the Pope and bishops.

26. Solicitor General—an official who had the duty of advising the different branches of English government on the law.

27. Tower of London—an ancient castle located in London on the shore of the River Thames. Built in 1078, it originally served as a royal residence. The castle was first used as a prison around the year 1100.

28. Vespers—the official Evening Prayer of the Church, consisting of psalms, a reading from Scripture, and intercessory prayers.

29. Viaticum—Holy Communion received by a person who is dying or is in danger of death.

Who are the Daughters of St. Paul?

We are Catholic sisters. Our mission is to be like Saint Paul and tell everyone about Jesus! There are so many ways for people to communicate with each other. We want to use all of them so everyone will know how much God loves them. We do this by printing books (you're holding one!), making radio shows, singing, helping people at our bookstores, using the Internet, and in many other ways.

Visit our website at www.pauline.org

Pauline BOOKS & MEDIA

The Daughters of St. Paul operate book and media centers at the following addresses. Visit, call, or write the one nearest you today, or find us at www.pauline.org.

CALIFORNIA
3908 Sepulveda Blvd, Culver City, CA 90230   310-397-8676
935 Brewster Ave., Redwood City, CA 94063   650-369-4230
5945 Balboa Avenue, San Diego, CA 92111   858-565-9181

FLORIDA
145 S.W. 107th Avenue, Miami, FL 33174   305-559-6715

HAWAII
1143 Bishop Street, Honolulu, HI 96813   808-521-2731

ILLINOIS
172 North Michigan Avenue, Chicago, IL 60601   312-346-4228

LOUISIANA
4403 Veterans Memorial Blvd, Metairie, LA 70006   504-887-7631

MASSACHUSETTS
885 Providence Hwy, Dedham, MA 02026   781-326-5385

MISSOURI
9804 Watson Road, St. Louis, MO 63126   314-965-3512

NEW YORK
64 West 38th Street, New York, NY 10018   212-754-1110

SOUTH CAROLINA
243 King Street, Charleston, SC 29401   843-577-0175

VIRGINIA
1025 King Street, Alexandria, VA 22314   703-549-3806

CANADA
3022 Dufferin Street, Toronto, ON M6B 3T5   416-781-9131